# Swedenborg
# & Gurdjieff:
## The Missing Links

SWEDENBORG & GURDJIEFF:
*The Missing Links*
Anti-Intuitive Essays for Personal Transformation

by Edward F. Sylvia, M. T. S.

ISBN: 978-0-9702527-2-2 (print)
        978-0-9702527-5-3 (kindle)

For information, contact:
        Staircase Press LLC
                www.StaircasePress.com
                books@staircasepress.com

Publisher's Cataloguing-In-Publication Data

Sylvia, Edward F.

        Swedenborg & Gurdjieff, the missing links : anti-intuitive essays for personal transformation / Edward F. Sylvia. -- Troy, IL : Staircase Press, c2012.

        p. ; cm.

        ISBN: 978-0-9702527-2-2
        Includes bibliographical references.
        Summary: An advanced course on the obstacles one faces and the special measures one must take to achieve spiritual growth. These strategies are distilled from the spiritual systems of Emanuel Swedenborg and George Gurdjieff. Intended for serious seekers of spiritual transformation.--Publisher.

        1. Swedenborg, Emanuel, 1688-1772. 2. Gurdjieff, Georges Ivanovitch, 1872-1949. 3. Transformative learning. 4. God--Proof from grades of perfection. 5. Spiritual life. I. Title.

BL624 .S95 2012
204/.4--dc23                                                    1205

# Swedenborg & Gurdjieff:
## The Missing Links

Anti-Intuitive Essays for Personal Transformation

Edward F. Sylvia, M.T.S.

STAIRCASE PRESS
ELEVATE YOUR MIND

*To all my family,*
*including those in the past*
*and in the future…*

## Other titles by the author:

**Sermon from the Compost Pile**
  Seven Steps Toward Creating An Inner Garden

**PROVING GOD**
  Swedenborg's Remarkable Quest for
  the Quantum Fingerprints of Love

  *2011 MONTAIGNE MEDAL WINNER*
  *honored as one of the most thought-provoking books of the year*

  *2011 ERIC HOFFER AWARD WINNER*
  *recognizing salient writing and independent spirit*

  *2011 SILVER NAUTILUS AWARD WINNER*
  *awarded to books that stimulate the imagination and*
  *offer new possibilities for a better life and a better world*

**COSMIC DUTY**
  A Swedenborgian's Interpretation of
  BEELZEBUB'S TALES TO HIS GRANDSON
  (All and Everything)

# Abbreviations:

These abbreviations are used as a key to specific books written by Emanuel Swedenborg that are referenced in the essays.

AC – *Arcana Coelestia* (Heavenly Secrets) 12 volumes

TCR – *True Christian Religion*

WLG – *The Worship and Love of God*

# TABLE OF CONTENTS

# Thorns & Roses

*"God grant me the serenity*
*to accept the things I cannot change,*
*the courage to change the things I can*
*and the wisdom to know*
*the difference."*

"*Self-observation brings man to the realization of the necessity of self-change. And in observing himself, a man notices that self-observation itself brings about certain changes in his inner processes. He begins to understand that self-observation is an instrument of self-change, a means of awakening.*"
~ *George Gurdjieff*

Like everything else inside this book, the fact that I'm the one writing the foreword surprised me at first. I'm not a scholar or an acknowledged "expert" in some lofty academic field of study. But as the author pointed out, I'm an expert on "him" and how his quest for Truth is affecting his life—and mine. If what he's written on these pages isn't put into action in his own life, he's failed. In sharing these ideas with you, he puts himself under the microscope. He asked me to "set it up and pull no punches." Here goes.

The content of this book has been the topic of many passionate and exhausting dinnertime and "over morning coffee" discussions in my home. I've known the author for 37 years and have witnessed the evolution of the material shared in these essays as it manifests in his own life. I'm delighted to see these insights finally take on an "essay" form in this book. If you read them, digest them and take them to heart, these insights could change your life, too. That's up to you, though. We all live in freedom.

"Everyday life" usually gets in the way of our best growth opportunities. Whatever hits us quickly gets our attention. That's why this is a skinny little book. It's a quick read. But don't be fooled. What you're holding in your hands is actually a really BIG book.

The author's curiousity and his passion for self-growth has made him a relentless lifelong seeker and student. I first met him at work 37 years ago. He was in his late twenties, kinda cute and had a "New York swagger" about him that belied his many inner insecurities. And he had some very unusal ideas about life. To a naïve young woman living in the midwest, he was "exotic." He was a student of Gurdjieff's work and actually used some of Swedenborg's ideas about eternal married love to woo me. How could I *not* be smitten?

We met in November and were married the following May. Whirlwind courtship? Probably. A week before the wedding, a mutual friend told me it would not last three years. What a lousy thing to say! That made me mad enough to hang in there *at least* three years, no matter what. In retrospect, it was probably the most constructive thing that anyone could have told me, because it made me "look beneath the surface" and examine my motives (as well as Ed's) continually through the years. It's been well worth the hassle.

As Ed shared all kinds of ideas I had never heard anywhere else before, I knew he was going to do something important someday. Or maybe something just plain crazy. He lives these ideas 24/7/365. It's his passion—his mission—to share what he has learned. And some of it sounds pretty weird at first blush.

Through the years, he has "met the requirements of life"—earning a living, raising a loving family, and living sustainably on a piece of land that is healthier and more vibrant now than when we first bought it some 30 years ago. All fine worldly accomplishments.

But honestly, none of that has ever been his first love. He did these things because he knew it was what one is "supposed to do" in this world. And sometimes it made him so miserable he took it out on everyone around him. I hung in there anyway, sensing that there was some greater purpose for all the conflict. Viewing difficult situations objectively and through the lens of Swedenborg's writings and Gurdjieff's work, we could both see that things seemed to "happen" for reasons greater than ourselves. So we'd work through things together. And we kept having wedding anniversaries.

36 years later, Ed is becoming a humble, wise man, but it wasn't always like that. There were some pretty rough years in there as he struggled with his inner demons, often letting them spill out into his interactions with other people. I was raised in a very traditional, peaceful and loving home and completely unaccustomed to the special brand of angst and drama that comes with what he calls "working on one's self." But we both felt there was "something there" worth striving for. We hung on for dear life and pretty much "saved" each other along the way. To this day, we're still very much a work in progress.

What most people never get to see is that he lives this process of "working on one's self" every waking hour of his life. He constantly "looks inside." His detractors have attacked him as being arrogant, egotistical, lazy, even cruel. Usually, because they are "uncomfortable" with something he has written. Or mad that he has not posted their snarky comment on his blog. (You would not believe some of the vicious comments that come to his blog. It amazes me how much venom otherwise "nice" people spew forth at each other on the internet. He does filter the worst of it for the sake of his readers.) On the other hand, he has engaged in intense, lengthy discussions with passionate priests, ministers, and laypeople; atheists and agnostics; Anglicans, Swedenborgians, Catholics and Jews; even scientists and card-carrying skeptics. And Swedenborg's and Gurdjieff's ideas continue to stand up under all the scrutiny. Best of all, most are genuinely grateful for what he shares so willingly.

Ed has always had a burning, heartfelt desire to observe and uncover the unsavory qualities in himself in order to try to change himself for the better. In many ways he's a walking lab experiment of the soul. His goal is to improve himself in this earthly life in order to have a better shot at an eternal place in heaven. It's a pretty unique way to approach every day. How can you *not* stay with someone like that and hope for the best?

I have actually learned a lot of coping skills along the way that have helped me make sense of my own life and allowed me to experience an inner peace that comes from understanding what really matters and what really doesn't. Seems to me that most of us focus most of our energy on a lot of the wrong stuff in life. In putting up with Ed's crap, I have hopefully begun to make some bit of progress on my own self. But there's still much work to be done—he puts up with a lot from me, too—and uses that to "work on himself." (Being offended or angry is really easy. *Truly forgiving isn't!*)

Even in his darkest times, there has always been an underlying passion for the insights he receives through study and reflection on the writings and teachings of Swedenborg and Gurdjieff. They seem to help us both make sense of the insanity of living in this terrestrial world. Before he started writing books, he would keep me up all night sometimes, sharing thoughts and ideas with me. (Sometimes talking "at" me, rather than "with" me, because he was so filled with things he needed to "put out there." He was like a fire hydrant pouring forth amazing ideas and insights.) Ed is a non-conformist, married to the queen of conformists. It has been a heck of an adventure for us both. (Some days I wish it was a little more boring!) To this day, I don't know for sure if we have "met in the middle" or if he's simply "coming into his own" and bringing me along for the ride. But we seem to be "becoming one."

In these essays he takes "the organized church" and "work groups" to task. Some will take offense at this. But he's not doing it to be "mean" or "disrespectful." These ideas have changed his life for the better and he has a deep desire to give back what he has received.

It's up to each of us to look beyond the surface, just like when my friend told me my marriage was destined to fail. If you let something *offend* you, that's really just *your reaction*. You can choose *not* to be offended, because when you think about it, being offended is really just your own ego getting in your way.

You can choose to wallow in self-righteous negativity and change nothing. Or you can also make the choice to *look inside yourself* and examine *what it is* about what you're hearing that's *really* making you uncomfortable. And as much as it pains "non-confrontational me" to say this, sometimes your own personal discomfort can be beneficial if you're open to observing your own reactions and learning something useful from the situation.

Neither of us was raised in the Swedenborgian church. We chose Swedenborg as adults because his writings resonated with us. Ed was attracted to Gurdjieff's work for the same reason. The two "schools of thought" really complement each other. We're not in church every Sunday morning, but when we are, the decision to go is made consciously and not out of habit. Ed is the only person I know who actually "gears up" for attending a Sunday service. When we get there, he doesn't sing the hymns and often seems to be in deep thought rather than participating in the service rituals. In reality, he's taking it all in very differently than the rest of us.

Ed's not a "small-talk" guy. But he loves nothing more than to dig into a God-focused conversation topic. If he connects with someone in a deep discussion, he'll hang in there as long as his conversation partner is willing to hang around. The exchange of ideas brings him to life. On a "good day," attending church can easily consume the entire Sunday for us. He is the only person I've ever met who will actually leave church exhausted.

For decades, he's been actively working on becoming a better person. On the other hand, I go busily through the motions of everyday life, making my daily commute and thinking little of flipping off the guy who just cut me off in traffic. All the while, it never occurs to me that I'm not a nice person. Hmm... that's rather scary. But Ed actually walks the talk, applying these ideas to his own life every day. While he sometimes seems gruff or insensitive on the outside, he's actually much kinder to others *from the heart* than I am. I've known him long enough and well enough to witness true transformation taking place. Swedenborg's and Gurdjieff's ideas are having a profound effect in him. Since he's been embracing this path and writing his books, I've seen him become more patient with people—and on those occasions when he does lose it, he catches himself and apologizes. He sincerely worries about people he can't "help" and prays for those who are in conflict with him. He's the most generous, honest person I have ever met.

His true life's work is to nudge people toward Truth. And sometimes Truth is not easy for us to hear. All this stuff has been refining itself inside him through most of his adult life. Scary and humbling as it's been for him sometimes, he's embracing a lot of personal changes as a result. And like it or not, life continues to serve up new "challenges" every time we conquer the last one.

With this book, his fire hydrant of spiritual insights is definitely open and flowing! Grab a bucket and drink in the wisdom, even though some of it isn't flattering.

These essays are short, but potent. They might make you uncomfortable. Actually, that's what he hopes will happen—for your own ultimate eternal benefit. The fragrant rose smells that much sweeter once you have conquered its thorns.

This little book is his heart on his sleeve. Hopefully you will find what you need here!

Be brave…

"In the spiritual body moreover,
man appears such as he is
with respect to love and faith,
for everyone in the spiritual world
is the effigy of his own love,
not only as to the face and the body,
but also as to the speech and the actions."
~ Emanuel Swedenborg

The harmonizing of two
dynamic spiritual systems
for the benefit of each

Woe is me.

I did not have fun writing these essays. They are sure to draw fire, even from long-time friends. But I cannot go to the grave remaining silent on some of the most important issues concerning the "human predicament."

To be blunt, we are all phonies.

Our phoniness is the general theme of these essays. (How's that for being anti-intuitive?) So to properly prepare you for this rude disclosure, there is an obvious need to share some important background setup info to get you familiar with where I am coming from.

I have been a student of the unique ideas of both Emanuel Swedenborg and George Gurdjieff for over thirty-five years. I have attended a Swedenborgian seminary, where I earned my MTS (Master of Theological Studies) and attended Gurdjieffian work groups in both New York and St. Louis. So I can legitimately discuss both approaches to spiritual evolution, their effectiveness, and unfortunately, some of my disappointments.

My disappointments are not with the ideas of these two great seers, but with the resulting cultures and biases created by their adherents over the passage of time. Both Swedenborg and Gurdjieff are dead, so those who have taken hold of the rudder are left with their personal navigational skills, which inevitably include some biases.

Back in 1993, after a Gurdjieff work group was finishing up a session, my teacher turned to me and said point blank, "Swedenborg can't help you." (She knew I also studied Swedenborg and several years earlier had warned me against discussing his ideas with her students without her direct permission.) While I inwardly recoiled at her curt statement, it propelled me on a journey to look more closely into the details of both Swedenborg's and Gurdjieff's systems of spiritual transformation—to understand why she would say this, and hopefully, in an objective and respectful way, prove her wrong.

My Gurdjieffian instructor was under the misguided impression that Swedenborg only offered ideas about cosmology—while Gurdjieff offered hands-on programs for his followers to obtain real inner growth. This judgment is technically true and easily concluded from the fact that Swedenborg did not take on pupils and oversee their personal development. But Swedenborg's cosmology, as well as Gurdjieff's, included human-kind's proper place and purpose in this created universe—which required a *special kind of effort to secure.* I had studied the ideas of both men since 1974 and they each addressed our God-given duty to challenge ourselves and rise above our habitual terrestrial lives.

Each system was designed to reveal our human phoniness and pretensions.

The question for me was whether or not Swedenborg's and Gurdjieff's systems took their followers equally *deep into the weeds.* Which system provided the best conditions for inner growth? It seemed to me, from both perspectives, that the question of our phoniness always remained the great big elephant in the room. What could be more awkward than a group of phonies who knew, on some level, they were indeed phonies, continuing to carry on deep philosophical and spiritual conversations?

Swedenborg assures us that even if we succeeded in becoming angels of the highest heaven, we would still be playing a role and acting "as if" good things originated from our own being, while inwardly, acknowledging that life, love and wisdom only comes from God. Gurdjieff described this challenging situation as *playing a role without inner identification.* So even in heaven, we can never completely let go of our sense of phoniness. (Even the Virgin Mary had to suffer this ultimate cosmic truth and personal indignity when Jesus called her "woman.")

This phoniness, my friend, is what we all have to ultimately come to grips with.

Our sense of "self" (called Proprium), relative to God, is an illusion. It is a necessary illusion, because without it we would feel deprived of life and not be in freedom to make life choices. But in the end we must still acknowledge our phoniness.

Only God has Proprium.

Ha, ha, ha, ha, ha, ha, ha, ha, ha, ha, ha, ha, ha, ha, ha, ha, ha, ha, ha, ha, ha, ha, ha, ha! What a pisser!

In other words, even if we are making real progress in spiritual growth, we still jump from one ridiculous condition to another. We will always be mere recipient forms of God's living influence—despite what our sensory organs are telling us. Awkward, yes, but for those who remain alert and brave, this acknowledgment can also bring us to a highly electrifying, highly liberating and consciousness-raising situation!

The difference between ignoble humans and candidates for God's heavenly kingdom is that the latter group uses pretense and phoniness to find humility and innocence, while the prior category uses it for deceit. Both Swedenborg and Gurdjieff address this sobering situation in uncomfortable detail.

In partial defense of my Gurdjieff leader, she was also faced with the real fact that my study of Swedenborg got in the way of a more focused commitment on my part to her own work group.

I did not share this same fear. I believed the two systems were complementary and helpful—well beyond what she might have believed.

Ever since I began studying the systems of these two great individuals I saw many powerful similarities in

their approach to spiritual or inner growth. I felt that
if I could merge both systems effectively, each would
benefit the other and as a result, their memberships
might increase through this osmosis. This would be
quite an undertaking since both systems required
grasping many unique and non-traditional ideas—
ideas expressed by the different writing styles of two
men living in different centuries. I believed that
universal principles—even if stated in different word
formulations and at different times—could be detected
by individuals who have made real efforts at striving
to think beyond mere memory-data, and from a loftier
principle of sincere spiritual love. (Love makes likeness
and unlikeness.)

For others not cultivating such a knack of perception,
tedious cross-translation would be necessary.

While a handful of individuals have indeed found it
useful to study both Swedenborg and Gurdjieff's ideas,
the two organizations tend to protect the purity of their
systems. Why should I care about their synthesis? Well,
my personal opinion is that both systems have stalled
in their attempts at influencing the rest of the world
with truly potent ideas. In a nutshell, they need each
other. But how could I prove this?

I certainly thought I had lots of ammo. But my "bullets"
usually bounced off their intended targets.

Whenever I would mention to other seekers in these
two camps that both Swedenborg and Gurdjieff had
cosmologies that included a non-material Spiritual Sun,
or that they both challenged human egoism, or that

they both had similar ideas called "remains" stored away in the *internal natural mind*, or that they both claimed spiritual growth (re-birth) required the devastation (vastation) of our former lives, or that they both touched on the phenomenon of hypnosis, or that Swedenborg's "Circle of Life" was analogous to Gurdjieff's "Enneagram," I would only receive a facial response of skepticism.

This skepticism led to my eventual self-banishment and exile from both organizations. However, I remained loyal to studying the revelations of both men!

Swedenborg made the eschatological claim that a "New Church" (The New Jerusalem) was now being established by the Lord upon the Earth. In the same vein, Gurdjieff confided in one of his followers that a "new school" was cosmically being established on Earth. These two statements made my antennae go up! A church is synonymous with a school because it is a place of instruction. But a church can atrophy if its worship becomes a mere observance of rituals, the singing of hymns and mundane fellowship. An esoteric school can atrophy if it loses sight of spiritual and theological considerations—that truth must lead to goodness and that goodness must lead to the Lord God.

I wondered if Swedenborg and Gurdjieff represented a providential and cosmic one-two punch by the Creator to get things off the dime and introduce new ideas to the world. My findings? Well, let me apologize ahead of time to my readers because some of my conclusions, while favorable to such a worldview, will be felt as a swift kick in the ass (which, if one is perfectly honest and has had actual encounters with their own phoniness, will understand that this is an essential ingredient towards legitimate personal transformation).

It seems to me that most of today's writers dealing with Swedenborg's or Gurdjieff's ideas have glossed over—and failed to emotionally communicate—the true horror of the current human predicament. They have all been timid at poking their sticks into a hornet's nest.

Not me.

Oh, I would like to add one more thing. Before the passing of my Gurdjieffian instructor (who was a pupil of Lord Pentland, the leader of Gurdjieff's movement in America), she gave me her permission to write a book that would compare the ideas of these unique spiritual leaders. I shared some preliminary writings with her, which she thought were good.

With that seal of approval, I will now tighten the screws. Or, more precisely, begin poking my stick into the hornet's nest.

# An Exodus from Symbolism?

Since spiritual transformation or regeneration operates through definite stages and lawful steps, I knew that if I submitted myself more intensely to this process I might identify just where the misunderstanding between the two approaches lies.

So as I studied Swedenborg's and Gurdjieff's ideas more deeply and put them into practice, I kept my eyes peeled. This "noble" undertaking may seem presumptuous to some of my readers, but be assured that I base any real success in this area only on my discovering something bitter—I succeeded in uncovering unflattering truths concerning the *rotten* and *savage* qualities of my inner spirit (which both Swedenborg and Gurdjieff said do need to be dug up and examined). These eye-opening self-discoveries are not what one normally brags about. But spiritual transformation requires that we compel and suffer ourselves to make these self-discoveries.

Yes, I *suffered* profound humiliation but did so *intentionally*! So I consider myself an expert in these "touchy" matters.

Terrestrial life only demands that we face the challenges of our ordinary, physical needs. Spiritual growth is an additional activity with additional demands. It involves a complete turnaround from our "normal" life and the complete reorganization of our knowledge and values. During spiritual development, the ideas collected in our memory during life begin to be ordered and oriented according to the higher principles and values (loves) we are choosing and adopting from both the world and theological influences. Therefore, I had complete confidence that if I could succeed in bringing some level of new and legitimate spiritual order into my own heart and mind, the ideas of the two men would find their proper placement, relative to each other, in my psyche (which is my spirit). I would not have begun such a lifelong venture if I had not intuitively sensed that the ideas of these two remarkable men would indeed harmonize.

This harmonization of ideas, to be successful, would have to extend all the way to holy secrets.

On the matter of holy secrets, this required the deciphering of profound symbolic and allegorical language, which was becoming a lost art even among spiritual seekers. I would also have to contend with a hardened post-modern worldview. In spite of the fact that scientists consider *metaphor* to be a sloppy method for finding truth, this would be one area that I fully intended to explore as a means of challenging their misguided assumptions about the structural nature of reality. (This modern assumption about metaphor and allegory is a direct outcome of naturalistic science—or scientism—leaving *values* and *divine order* out of their methodology for describing the real world.)

Gurdjieff, like Swedenborg, embraced symbolism as
a lawful means of exploring reality that was beyond
the reach of the five senses. Metaphor allows the mind
to grasp the hidden world from things known and
observed in the visible world—they correspond as a
result of divine, top-down, fine-tuning throughout
creation. In other words, both men believed that lower
levels of reality were perfectly analogous to higher,
metaphysical or spiritual levels of reality. This type
of symbolism is perfectly scientific and Swedenborg
called it the *science of correspondences*. However,
harmonizing the symbolic expressions of these two
men wasn't going to be easy. Gurdjieff seemed to use
symbols in a more shocking manner. For instance, back
in the early 1980s, I was intellectually confounded by
a carving on a wooden door leading to a "sacred move-
ments" room at a Gurdjieff Center that my work group
was visiting near San Francisco. The carving contained,
among other things, a depiction of a devil and angel
as opposite but important forces within our spiritual
development. Even though Swedenborg revealed that
the Lord God providently used evil to preserve our
psychic equilibrium and free will, Gurdjieff used the
concepts of evil and good in a more unexpected theological manner to describe the universal processes of
"involution" and "evolution" and how they related to
our spiritual challenge.

Years later (and with greater understanding) I could see
how this unusual symbolic idea actually agreed with
Swedenborg's concept of *influx*, and that if one was
spiritually lazy and not vigilant, this influx, as it flowed

downward (involution) from heaven into the hearts and minds of men and women on earth, would eventually be twisted into its opposite value and leaks out as flawed behavior. (This twisting is the result of the human will being totally perverted and corrupted.)

To help you get a more visceral sense of this *twisting* and *leaking* of energy it will be most helpful to point out that it manifests in our lives as mechanicality, suggestability, daydreaming, egoism, negativity, irritation, anger, impatience, self-indulgence and in fretting about our social status and reputation (internal considering). We all exhibit these flawed traits, yet we easily ignore them as a sign that something is indeed fundamentally askew and abnormal in our lives or that we are recklessly squandering God's life force.

The human race has a cosmic responsibility to prevent this downward trend from continuing to "leak" into questionable behavior. The "Devil" in Gurdjieff's system represents the downward flow (involution) of living force from God into the wrongly-formed minds of worldly men, while the "Angel" represents a reversal of forces or an upward trajectory (evolution) by humans noticing something wrong in themselves and making a conscious choice to aspire to higher, spiritual conditions. Therefore the downward flow—away from God and into the physical world—could indeed be represented by a devil, while the upward flow— towards God—is best represented, of course, by an angel. These two forces (also called passive and active) were in eternal opposition, yet one needed the other!

So, without an understanding of sacred symbolism, the individual is limited in his or her search for helpful knowledge and the perennial philosophy offered by the Creator. For instance, my suffering of humiliation that I described at the beginning of this essay is symbolized in the Bible by the eating of unleavened bread (puffiness from the action of yeast symbolizes the magnified human ego and self-importance).

Grasping symbolism is not a function of ordinary or habitual living. It is evidence of a *non-ordinary* (holotropic) state of consciousness by which a person opens up his or her higher functions of mind and becomes sensitive to otherwise inaccessible information. These higher functions are purely spiritual and contain angelic wisdom but are dormant during normal terrestrial living. Opening these higher functions of mind takes both effort and a special kind of volitional suffering by which we challenge our own egoism. (The problem here is that most people believe their ordinary consciousness to be fine and dandy and that symbolism provides no practical value in their daily lives and struggles.)

(In his book *Meetings With Remarkable Men*, Gurdjieff describes being amazed that the epic Sumerian tale of Gilgamesh was passed to him orally before the tablets containing this pre-biblical story of the Flood were ever unearthed. He regretted not having studied ancient myths more intensely. He did, however, seem to be well acquainted with the Bible, and that ancient writers used a symbolic language called "podobolizovany" or "making alike" [Correspondences] in their storytelling. Also, he seemed at home deciphering the symbolic language of the prehistoric cave paintings in Lascaux, France.)

In spite of the fact that Swedenborg claimed that God's Holy Word contained symbolic, or higher levels of meaning (and he offered more than a dozen books worth of evidence), the Swedenborgian Church seemed (from my point of view) to be downplaying this potent aspect of their doctrines and the existence of holy secrets. (Ironically, I met people who were not church-goers, but were hungry for this symbolic, spiritual teaching.) This situation was a concern for me because these higher meanings in Scripture were what attracted me to this church in the first place. I took steps to make sure this concern was not merely a product of my subjective or wild-ass imagination—so I waited for an appropriate moment to ask for an "official" response to this concern of mine.

About 18 years after being told "Swedenborg could not help me," I was having dinner with a Swedenborgian scholar and asked him point blank if "the Swedenborgian Church is walking away from correspondences?" (Again, correspondences are the particular symbolic language and system of allegory that Swedenborg claimed would allow one to obtain deeper meanings from the stories in Holy Scripture. Inwardly, the Bible narratives are more than mere historical accounts of humankind's past, and contain important and deeper details concerning salvation and God's eternal activities. In other words, correspondences were the only legitimate means for accessing holy secrets.)

My Swedenborgian academic acquaintance finally replied *"Not really, but the church is focusing on simple goodness."*

Bingo!

# Being "GOOD" May Not Be So GOOD

My academic friend's answer told me that Swedenborgian leaders, probably faced with shrinking membership, pragmatically chose to simplify their message.

Somewhere along the line it was acknowledged that while the language of correspondences is difficult to teach and learn, the concept of "goodness" could be easily taught and understood by every Tom, Dick and Sally. Furthermore, even a casual reading of Swedenborg's theological writings shows that they are centered on the *Doctrine of Love* and *usefulness*.

The purpose of God's truth and teachings is to lead us to *goodness*. So, why not emphasize goodness and go directly for the tasty, low-hanging fruit? Duh!

To challenge this highly rational theological maneuver would make me come off as a seriously misguided (if not mischievous) soul. To be honest, however, I saw this strategy as a "dumbing-down" of the Lord's new dispensation—made available through Swedenborg's vast visionary efforts and theological writings, which spanned three decades. I am not insensitive to the fact that few people today have the time to absorb all this potent information (or more cynically, perhaps they suffer from laziness). The important question is: why would Swedenborg have written so many scholarly books if his message was to simply tell us to be good people? Heck, the guy down the street can tell me that!

I personally believe that besides life's worldly challenges taking up more of people's time there is also a misguided assumption, buried deep within people's noggins, that we modern exemplars of the human race are somehow more "evolved" than those who lived in former times. This permits us to keep our guard down—especially towards anything that may seem out-of-whack according to our modern self-images of ourselves.

But it is worse than that! We suffer real cognitive degeneration!

As I mentioned previously, both Swedenborg and Gurdjieff recognized the importance of symbolism and allegory in ancient traditions—*for the purpose of elevating the human mind*. And, both visionaries made the unflattering claim that ancient civilizations actually enjoyed a more highly developed intellect than we currently do! While Gurdjieff harped on this topic a bit more often than Swedenborg, quotes agreeing with this demeaning premise can indeed be found in Swedenborg's writings. Such as:

*"Those who were of the ancient church, and especially those of the most ancient, were much wiser than the men of our times..."* (AC 6876)

And the reason for this superior intelligence was the symbolic knowledge of correspondences.

Swedenborg states:

*"How much the ancients surpassed the moderns in intelligence can be seen from the fact that they knew to what things in heaven many things in the world correspond, and consequently what they signify..."* (AC 7729[8])

This is the reason why I asked the question about the study of correspondences among current Swedenborgian organizations (churches). The focus of these organizations on *love* and *goodness* seems theologically solid but it has actually led to a strategic mistake!

Swedenborg makes it clear that God's loving mercy, while constant, cannot save us without our cooperation. A simple analogy would be to describe our situation as that of a full glass of dirty water. We each have to spill some of this dirty water out to make room for God's purified water (truth) to pour in. This pouring out of dirty water is called repentance. (AC 9014)

The mistake can also be illustrated on a triangular graphic (as shown on the following page). Seeking love or goodness *directly* actually limits the inner trine (or triad) of a person's involvement and can lead to incomplete or lopsided spiritual growth! Why think in terms of trines? Because "trines" represent universal, cosmic laws.

Swedenborg (as well as Gurdjieff) insisted that three elements or forces (threefoldness) where always needed to create anything. This threefold requirement also applies to our spiritual growth. The three universal aspects that combine to form all things are described as *active* force, *passive* force, and *reconciling* force (which are analogous to the Holy Trinity). God's Love (as the Father) enters as "active" force into the soul and mind of humans. God's truth (Son) acts as a "passive" force and enters through the external senses from hearing or reading God's Holy Word. (The reason why truth acts as a passive force is because it puts constraints on love and gives love its boundaries, extent and quality.) A person's will acts as a third force and determines how the active and passive influences are to be *conjoined* (neuro-nuptials) through our actions. This produces a "good deed" (useful result) in the world. (If one's will is appropriately spiritual the Holy Spirit assists and proceeds through it to form a more noble reconciling principle.) This threefold process or trine produces an outer effect like the one illustrated below:

*Figure 1:* **First Trine**

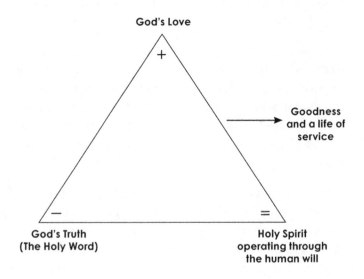

When a church rushes to promote "goodness," people prematurely envision themselves under the law of this particular trine (shown here). On the surface of things, what more could one want to obtain from a church teaching or church worship? But this is an incomplete strategy and can lead to counterfeit acts of goodness! Actually, a further determination of one's spiritual quality or the quality of one's heart is still needed.

We have to be tested. Here's why:

For a trine to produce *genuine* goodness within a life of service (instead of phoniness) it must do more than bring a benefit to some other person or to society. It must lead to the salvation of the person doing the good deed. Here is where the subject of goodness gets more complicated than most people suspect or are taught. In order for the knowledge of God's truths or tenets (passive force) to be properly conjoined with divine good (active force) from heaven, this conjunction must be made on a more interior level of the human natural mind where elements of our dark side are hiding. (To ignore this dark side is self-deception.) If spiritual knowledge is not directed *inwards* to confront this dark side, it simply stays put as mere "memory-data," which can be manipulated by a deceitful and unrepentant will (hidden agenda or subtext). After all, a scheming politician can lead a life of service and show outward acts of goodness.

The proper interior conjunction (marriage) of God's goodness and truth in the human psyche should not simply produce acts of service as shown in *Figure 1*, but also the growth of spiritual *conscience*, which can now bring a person under the conditions of a *different trine.* Spiritual conscience represents a plane or boundary within the human psyche where heaven can flow in and establish itself. It is from this *plane of conscience* (also called by Swedenborg "remains") that God forms a new trine in us for the purpose of genuine salvation and spiritual growth.

During legitimate spiritual regeneration, *goodness* and *truth* now combine as an active force in the human psyche but is now put up against a whole new type of passive or resisting force called *evil* compulsions— that is, *temptations.* As mentioned previously, these compulsions represent an unchecked downward trajectory called involution. The third (reconciling) force of this new trine is *conscience.* And if it is truly good, the resulting activity (battle) within a person's will successfully connects one's outer physical activities and service with the spiritual activity and inner quality of one's evolving spirit.

*Figure 2:* **Second Trine**

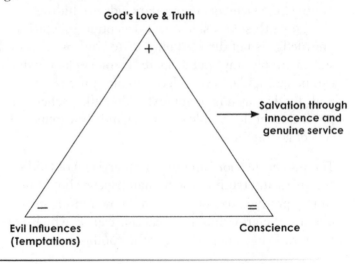

**God's Love & Truth**

+

Salvation through innocence and genuine service

−

Evil Influences
(Temptations)

=

Conscience

A life of service (goodness) does not guarantee salvation. Opposition is necessary to qualify our actions and deeds. This is the only way for goodness to acquire innocence, where it becomes genuinely spiritual.

Both Swedenborg and Gurdjieff treated human *genuineness* as suspect. And they both took extreme actions in their own lives to remedy their own shortcomings by means of this second trine.

It is my belief that the Swedenborgian Church, in its effort to simplify things, has *prematurely* gravitated to the first trine (goodness+truth+human will = result) while my experience with Gurdjieffians has showed me that they are focused on the second, more difficult trine (goodness+evil+conscience = genuine result)!

However, through my careful reading of both men's writings I have found that they each address both trines shown above. Both trines are important to contemplate, but we cannot exchange one for another in order to make our spiritual challenges seem easier. Gurdjieff admits that his methods for personal transformation are quite difficult while Swedenborg expresses a similar difficulty by claiming that few people on earth are currently brought into states of real temptation— because their egoism makes them ill-equipped to handle such inner challenges. This challenge is symbolized by Jesus' words that He had many more things to reveal but that His listeners could not "bear these things now." (John 16:12)

What could we not bear?

Further biblical support for this harsh assessment is provided by the strange event of John eating a small book or scroll *(Revelation 10:9, 10)*. At first it tasted sweet, but later became bitter in his belly. The lesson in these verses cannot be explained without the knowledge of sacred symbolism. God's precepts (the scroll) first seem "sweet" to us but after digesting these laws more deeply and applying them to our actual lives (eating symbolizes appropriation) they become sour— becasue our inner flaws are made known to us.

True spiritual advancement requires swallowing a "bitter pill."

The
Spiritual
Sun

Gurdjieff and Swedenborg both claimed that there is a righteous sun at the center of all the activity in the universe.

Both spiritual pioneers also claimed that this unique cosmic concentration is the *eternal abode* of the Lord God in heaven. Swedenborg called it the *Spiritual Sun* while Gurdjieff called it the *Most, Most Holy Sun Absolute.*

The "light" from this Holy psycho-spiritual Sun is why we can close our eyes and see our ideas. It provides the intellectual light for our mind's eye and spirit.

Swedenborg suggests that contemporary scientists will never be able to formulate a correct model or theory of reality or of creation without acknowledging the existence and influence of the Spiritual Sun in the universe. (This is why modern science is stuck with the nonsensical idea that the universe was created out of nothing.) Gurdjieff, like Swedenborg, stated that the physical sun (second order sun) derives its origin from the non-material sun of the spiritual world. Both men claimed this primal sun (the first proceeding influence from God's activity) to be *living* and *organic.* Its conscious activity is responsible for all processes in the universe, from creation to evolution to salvation.

In Swedenborg's theological writings, this sun illuminates and warms the higher domain of spirits and angels. This heat and light is *non-physical* (Theo-dynamics rather than thermodynamics). It represents God's enlightening truth and warming love, which sustains the angels (and everything below).

Gurdjieff stated in his epic book *Beelzebub's Tales To His Grandson* that the Sun Absolute ruled the *Protocosmos* or primal world and that individuals with perfected higher-being bodies (vessels for the soul) could return to and re-blend with this original source of creation. The Protocosmos is Gurdjieff's terminology for God's heavenly kingdom. (Gurdjieff no doubt used this terminology to break through the stiff language of current theological dogma and put heaven within a more rational, cosmological framework.)

The proper return to this primal holy source of creation requires that an individual gain the ability to embrace and metabolize the sacred data emanating from the Sun Absolute itself. This sacred data is the knowledge of God's love and truth, which represents the energy source and the real food of the human spirit, including those who have evolved into angels. (That is why we thirst for truth and hunger for love.)

The metabolism of this sacred data is analogous to individuals accepting and following the Lord's tenets and commandments and living a spiritual life. But this higher form of digestion (appropriation) can go much further than mere obedience to divine law if we continue to elevate the mind! The further upward (or inward) movement of our hearts and minds brings us closer to the activity of God's Spiritual Sun.

One of the outcomes of *willfully* coming under greater and greater influence from this non-material Sun is that an individual's mind is eventually opened up to understand the symbolic language of angels—which is to view everything from the light of *correspondences*. Failing to do so creates a culture (as I mentioned earlier) that begins to falsely believe that it is more intelligent and evolved than those of more ancient times. The advancement of worldly technology and science buttress this false opinion of our cognitive progress. Again:

*"How much the ancients surpassed the moderns in intel-ligence can be seen from the fact that they knew to what things in heaven many things in the world correspond, and consequently what they signify..."* (AC 7729[8])

Furthermore, as the augmented metabolism necessary for digesting symbolic language takes place in our minds; a parallel re-birth can occur in the formation of a more subtle spiritual body developing within a person's gross physical body. (New spiritual functions and sensitivities require that new spiritual organs develop within us.) Swedenborg states:

*"Now the spiritual body must be formed in the mate-rial body, and is formed by means of truths and goods which, flowing in from the Lord through the spiritual world, are received by man interiorly in such things in him as are from the natural world, which are called civil and moral. It is evident, therefore, what must be the nature of its formation."* (TCR 583)

The Swedenborgian Church may not think that its members need to explore such theological topics so deeply, but such a decision can only hinder their organization's ability to morph into the Lord's New Jerusalem and become the "crown of all churches" (which is the Lord's intent). I have never heard any Swedenborgian talk about the creation of spiritual bodies during the coffee hour after church.

I believe more serious thought must be given to the formation of higher being-bodies during the process of spiritual re-birth. We cannot passively hope that the subject will someday be covered in a sermon or that this simply becomes "someone else's responsibility." It is the development of the spiritual body that allows one to live in the spiritual realm and not suffer the "roasting" effects of God's intense love and wisdom emanating from the Spiritual Sun. Because of this oversight, the average Swedenborgian churchgoer has acquired a more pedantic and self-delusional notion of what happens when the Lord and his Spiritual Sun moves closer into a person's life. I know this because most people want to believe that during such a close sacred encounter, one will be bathed in resplendent love.

Not so.

Gurdjieff states that such a close encounter with the Sun Absolute will actually bring *remorse* to the individual. After all, something with greater purity than our own is bound to reveal our shortcomings during any encounter. Swedenborg won't try to soothe us here, either. He declares that the Spiritual Sun's increased presence and proximity in our lives will actually disturb and activate the evil compulsions in our impure nature. In this way, the Spiritual Sun exposes the impurities of our heart and mind— things that God cannot cuddle-up to.

I have found that stressing mere goodness in the church tends to make its worshippers believe that as God and the Spiritual Sun approaches and affects their lives, they will experience a heart-warming celestial cuddle and spiritual euphoria, rather than a proper inner purging. But how else can someone have genuine humility forged into their psyche without purging?

Threatened by my taking a hard line on this matter, I have also had serious-thinking Swedenborgians remind me that Swedenborg stated that a person need merely search out one or more personal evils (TCR 566) or examine one's evils once or twice a year. (TCR 621[6]) I counter this with Swedenborg's statements that we should purge ourselves before partaking of Holy Communion and that he who leads a life of faith does repentance daily. (AC n 8391) What this gradation of intensity means is that everyone can get off at his or her exit!

Another favorite comment is that Swedenborg made it perfectly clear that "Leading a heaven-bound life is not as hard as people believe." (A statement taken from Chapter 55 of Swedenborg's most popular book *Heaven and Hell*.) However, this hardship is based on a false premise many people have that one must completely

renounce the world in order to become spiritual.
But both Swedenborg and Gurdjieff stressed that one
must stay involved with worldly life. *We must evolve
spiritually from where we are*—not on some mountain
or in an isolated monastery. Swedenborg's point was
that nobody is incapable of living a civil or moral life.
And nobody is incapable of spiritual love and goodness.
But indeed, something must be difficult in our getting
there—or the world would be a much different place.

The difficulty is that legitimate spiritual evolution
requires a lot of "balloon-popping"! While this is easy
for the mind to acknowledge, it is extremely difficult
for the human heart.

This leads to a "fiery" battle. (AC 8403[2])

Sorry.

# REGENERATION AND HIGHER BEING-BODIES

Because attending worship service is at the heart of the Swedenborgian experience, most members easily overlook the biological and structural aspects of spiritual re-birth.

This is another downside to the clergy simplifying the message and simply challenging a congregation to be *good*. Swedenborgians who want to discuss deeper topics (and the actual obstacles in the path toward spiritual goodness) must do so through gatherings and groups arranged at other times of the week— never in Sunday church service!

*Worshippers cannot be made uncomfortable in any way.* (Even when the topic of evil is discussed, it seems to me to be fully neutered and de-clawed. I call this theological castration.)

Congregations are also to blame. I know of ministers who have been thrown out on the street if they did not treat their members with kid gloves and promote only "cheerfulness." Yet, intellectually, everyone nods approvingly when they are told that *irritation* is what causes an oyster to make a pearl.

What this all means is that worship service, rejoicing and the fellowship of the church community is now more central to the Swedenborgian experience than regeneration—especially its bio-details.

But this is simply a cultural trajectory to conform to the ecclesiastical crowd, to current social sensitivities, to act predictably "church-ish" and serve people's growing addiction to cheerfulness—rather than an institution for serious *regeneration*. (Cheerfulness is a good thing as long as we don't seek it to cover over our inner nullity—which is shockingly confirmed during genuine spiritual transformation. Also, cheerfulness and joy are proper outcomes of successfully getting past some personal stage of inner challenge—not *before* or *instead of*.) Here is what Swedenborg stated about the theological incompleteness of simply embracing good actions (at the expense of making people inwardly uncomfortable).

*"The church has indeed been set up anew with a man when he does what is good from affection; but still it has not been fully set up anew until he has fought against evil and falsities, thus until he has endured temptations; after this he becomes truly a church..."* (AC 6658)

Again:

*"... For spiritual life is acquired through temptations..."* (AC 8346)

Even those who attend church seeking the Lord's mercy still cannot skip this painful step:

*"The mercy of the Lord is perpetual with every man, for the Lord wills to save all men, whoever they are; but this mercy cannot flow in until evils have been removed..."* (AC 8307)

Swedenborg admits that he did not attend church often himself, and more importantly, refutes the central importance of church service alone, stating that the Lord does not need our praise and that true worship is following the commandments while faithfully being useful to others in our daily lives.

True worship is a matter of the way we live, not the way we bend our knees or clasp our hands and pray. In fact, Swedenborg is quite blunt in his *Arcana Coelestia* (Secrets of Heaven n 8179) that even prayer is no substitute for the inner pain and suffering from temptations and the spiritual combat required in the process of regeneration (God creating a new will inside our psyche). But again, simply attending church can give us the illusion that we are becoming good people while increasing our bio-ignorance of the actual process of true salvation.

Bio-ignorance?

Swedenborg states that the reason for creation is that the Lord God wants to create a heavenly kingdom from the human race. Becoming angels is the true trajectory of God's design for human evolution. Both Swedenborg and Gurdjieff insist that bio-structure and organic considerations are not absent in this angelic trajectory.

Heaven is teeming with life. Therefore, it is the lawful extension of the earth's biosphere into a non-material, theological realm. Spirits and angels living in this realm of eternal happiness also have real, substantive bodies. These bodies are formed from spiritual and mental substances and are the continued bio-results of living according to God's precepts. Our life choices allow God's tenets to become fixed within the depths of our very bio-fabric.

Life, even in heaven, cannot exist without coherent forms. During spiritual transformation our noble affections of love and its ideas—which are real spiritual substances—are not just fixed into our very being; they are distinguished into *genera, species* and *particulars,* and form both our spiritual environment as well as the organs, tissues and fibers of our spiritual bodies! (We can fathom this multi-leveled organic reality because everything in the physical body refers to some actual part of the brain, and everything in the brain refers to some actual thought, passion or activity of the mind. That means the mind and spirit have human form, and everything below are analogs of the human form— otherwise there would be no possible connection or consistency between our various levels of life.)

This rarefied bio-structure (the fixing of God's teachings into our very being and bio-fabric) provides a more sublime *body suit* for the soul and allows spirits and angels to live and work on a higher plane of reality with all the organic functions and amenities they had while living on earth. To quote Swedenborg again on this matter, let me repeat what was said in Essay 3:

*"Now the spiritual body must be formed in the material body, and is formed by means of truths and goods which, flowing in from the Lord through the spiritual world, are received by man interiorly in such things in him as are from the natural world, which are called civil and moral. It is evident, therefore, what must be the nature of its formation."* (TCR 583)

Unlike our gross physical body, which comes from the genetic contributions of our earthly parents, the spiritual body comes from God. It consists of our chosen values and understanding (which are real substances and forms that are capable of incubating a new bio-angelic person). It is well known that a person's understanding is determined by how well he or she can rationally arrange the ideas in their memory. What is less known is that this arrangement (body of knowledge) takes on an actual organic structure. What else could house the human soul but our deepest values and ideas forming our very living fabric? What else could form the spiritual organs necessary for processing God's love and truth in heaven? This spiritual bio-structure determines what placement in the spiritual world our hearts and minds will be adapted to—good or bad.

God's justice moves *inwards and organically.*

Without taking organic process into account, religion merely becomes an exercise in distorted hope and keeping one's head in the clouds. Swedenborg is adamant that it is from these very same clouds of our mental obscurity that the Lord will attempt to bust through and make His grand "second" appearance by revealing secret things through the knowledge of correspondences. This means that the Lord intends to shake things up—not on Earth, but in our hearts and minds with potent new information that throws light on our behavior. Personal salvation and the Second Coming of the Lord, are, the same thing! The symbolic language of correspondences in Holy Scripture reveals this unified concept while glorifying the Lord God!

As mentioned earlier, I have sadly experienced that few people want to discuss the details of these or other esoteric topics during the coffee hour after church services. Furthermore, few worshippers even make a regular study of Swedenborg's writings and prefer to be spoonfed by the minister's sermons—after all, that is what ministers get paid for. Worse, people have complained to me in church that when I bring these deeper topics up, that most interest me, I make them feel dumb and inadequate—which is a social no-no these days.

Ironically, sitting in a church pew puts one smack dab into a rich environment of symbols and secret knowledge. The candles, altar, music, the liturgy—even the placement of things either to the right or the left within this sacred space—contain powerful spiritual meanings. Understanding these symbols allows one to more deeply penetrate and appreciate church rituals!

In P. D. Ouspensky's book, *In Search of the Miraculous,* he recounts Gurdjieff telling him that the liturgy and rituals of the Christian Church were first taken from ancient Egypt. This means that all worship originally contained profound symbolic meaning (correspondences), cultivated by those in the know. Swedenborg seems to confirm this by his statement that:

*"… the Egyptians were versed in the knowledge of the rituals of the church above the rest who constituted the representative church after the time of the flood. At that time all rites were representative of spiritual things which are in heaven."* (AC 7779[4])

Little does a congregation take into account that when they are asked by a minister during the church service to "please stand up," it represents a reminder that they are to *elevate their minds*. Rather, I end up having to endure listening to their worldly concerns and "chit-chatting" after church service—in the name of Christian community and fellowship.

My life is not so long that I can waste chunks of it.

I was once even warned that I would no longer be allowed into church if I continued to pursue subjects which caused any discomfort to the congregation. Unfortunately, affirmation is trumping Truth.

To be fair-minded, Swedenborgians, with their vast esoteric teachings, have a real fear of coming off as a cult or being called New Age "Gnostics" (not mainstream and non-traditional). This is why I have detected a shy-ness in the Swedenborgian Church for promoting their true uniqueness. In fact, Swedenborgian ministers rarely toot their horn outside of their own church walls.

One current church strategy for growth, again based on "goodness," seems to be the promotion of "Pluralism" or "Universalism" and an acceptance of all faith systems. Swedenborg's theological writings seem to favor this doctrinal position of universal acceptance and love. But Swedenborg also went beyond mere equality!

Swedenborg observed that all faith systems do indeed play a role in heaven—much like *the different organs in the human body* perfect unity through a diversity of functions. But he also stated that special representatives of these various faiths are further educated by angels concerning the Lord's highest truths and in turn, are always sharing these advanced teachings with those members of their particular faiths who are inclined to listen and learn new things.

In spite of worldly political correctness, there are hierarchies in heaven. While God gives his love equally to all, not all people accept or receive this love equally. Also, those individuals who transcend the limitations of their own faith systems have eternal abodes more deeply placed within heaven—just like the neurons and nerve fibers constitute a deeper level of structure within the human organs, vessels and tissues.

Heaven's societies and commerce take on all the details of a grand human form—which is the Lord God's likeness and image. God is divinely and infinitely human!

the
"remains"

Swedenborg's doctrine of "remains" is not found anywhere else in Christian theology. (I have yet to find it expressed in the other major religions, either.)

Amazingly, Gurdjieff seems to describe a similar concept.

Basically, as each of us enters the world at birth and enjoys the pampering of early childhood, the Lord carefully stores away our tender experiences of love, innocence and the supportive words from our parents and teachers deep within our *inner natural mind*. Here, this sacred gift from God is kept safe from the later allurements and vanities of the world when we grow older.

This sacred "residue" or collection of innocent qualities is what makes us human in that it provides a plane for God's angelic influence to get a foothold into our psyche. (Gurdjieff stated that a child's love for his or her parents provides a place for God to enter.) This matrix is used later by the Lord during the *process* of our *spiritual bio-growth* and provides divine *opposition* to our evil tendencies and negative compulsions, which are oriented to egoism, self-indulgence and love of worldly power, reputation and rank. The resulting *contact* and *conflict* between these opposing values determines the extent we allow our remains to grow and mature into a new bio-structure and spiritual reality. The health and development of our remains is equal to the quality and development of one's conscience (remember the importance of conscience in the second trine in Essay #2).

This is new information—many Swedenborgians have not yet made the connection between the remains and spiritual conscience or with the remains and new biostructure. And Gurdjieffians would benefit from knowing how the sacred data of conscience is stored in the subconscious mind.

Conscience is an inner dictate based on a deep perception of truth. The Lord God implants this sensitivity as a "starter kit" in our remains. We must play an active part in its further development into a spiritual conscience and inner body.

In the Seven-Day Creation Story of Genesis, Swedenborg stated that *God's spirit moving across the faces of the waters* symbolically signified the "awakening" of these remains deep within our subconscious mind—which starts our spiritual re-birth. The emergence of dry land and its transformation into a garden paradise symbolizes the bio-evolution of our remains into spiritual wisdom. Thus, the Genesis story in Scripture symbolizes, on a deeper level, the *epigenesis* of the human heart and mind or one's spiritual *re-creation*.

It took years of studying Gurdjieff to realize that he had a similar idea to Swedenborg's "remains." (This ought to get some people's attention!) Gurdjieff simply described it as "Sacred Data" placed in one's subconscious mind from "Above." He, too, described this sacred data as providing the matrix that would eventually form *spiritual conscience*. (In earlier lectures Gurdjieff described this special sacred data as *magnetic center*.) *Our spiritual evolution can only proceed from our "remains,"* for without something holy stored up within us, we would have nothing concrete to start from or build upon.

But something bad happens along the way that cuts us off from our remains. In the *Arcana Coelestia* (AC 8247), Swedenborg supports Gurdjieff's claim that we learn to divide our minds for the sake of pretense in childhood.

Both Swedenborg and Gurdjieff claimed that as we grow up and learn from the world how to lie to others, and even lie to ourselves, this is what actually drives the sacred residue (remains) of our essential life "underground," where it becomes a subconscious function. (Swedenborg's *inner natural man* is the same as the human subconscious mind of Gurdjieff's teaching.) Not only does the sacred essential function of our remains actually get covered over by a new outer and worldly personality that takes shape and functions purely from memory data, so does the unregenerate *animus* (affection of the cerebrum) get driven under as well.

As a result of this new *outer coating* of the psyche, which is a fabrication, we are left with nothing real to work with for our spiritual evolution—not our remains, nor our hurtful proclivities, which are all put out of conscious reach.

*People are inwardly asleep and outwardly mechanical.* So we can only count on our God-given remains to counter our egoism up to a certain point.

Gurdjieff states that this takeover by a new corporeal/ worldly personality from continuous acts of self-deceit becomes, by habit, a second nature—that is something artificial and mechanical, responding chiefly by external stimuli. Swedenborg calls this division of the psyche into a new mechanical and artificial state "pulmonary thought." So we create this split in our psyche from the abnormal life and pressures of "fitting-into" the disharmonies of modern society.

*"This division of the natural man into two forms is an actual division of both will and thought, for all a man's actions proceed from the will, and all his speech from the thought. A second will is formed ... this second will which is formed by the man may be called his corporeal will, because it moves the body to act morally; and his second thought may be called pulmonary thought."* (TCR 593).

As a result of this division, our external actions in the world can be quite different from what our inner reality actually wills and thinks. This is the origin of hypocrisy and deceit in the human race.

The *internal natural man* is who we really are, but again, from the abnormalities of habitual terrestrial life, ends up underneath this second mind or new personality (like a seed and its germplasm surrounded by a husk). Both Swedenborg and Gurdjieff insisted that the internal or subconscious mind is what needs to be regenerated first because that is what houses our essential nature with its evil intentions. Gurdjieff described our second, fabricated outer personality as containing *everything in it except oneself.* (To simply change the second or outer personality is like changing masks.)

Worse yet, the second or fabricated personality intercepts all valuable information coming from the senses and prevents it from reaching (penetrating) our essential nature—where it is most needed to help our remains grow into a new spiritual being.

Sincere self-examination is what cuts through this barrier! Self-deception destroys one's remains.

Interestingly, we have our spiritual remains in the same vicinity (interior natural mind) as our deepest worldly and selfish motives (inherited evils)—both encrusted over by our habitual and fabricated corporeal mind. According to Swedenborg, the Lord stealthily insinuates the remains among our many inherited evils and falsities (AC 576). This is a most interesting strategy by God! During spiritual growth and self-examination our remains get activated into a psycho "turf war" with our deepest negative qualities within our interiors. The resulting turf war rearranges the map and boundaries of our inner bio-reality.

This is why we cannot simply decide one day to be "good." It does not get at the heart of the matter (made difficult by our divided mind). In order for goodness not to be superficial or provide us with just a new mask to hide behind, the inner natural mind (which is our essential being) must be brought into the process of change.

Let me again set the stage for you. The interiors of our natural mind is the psycho-turf or mental plane where our deepest evil tendencies reside, and is where our God-given remains are safely kept. These influences cannot live side-by-side forever and one of them must ultimately emerge as the victor. But these opposing influences usually operate below the radar of our habitual mind, and don't make profitable contact without a conscious decision from the heart. This life-changing decision requires each of us to fearlessly engage in the sincere self-examination of our intentions and to willfully suffer the contact between our conflicting influences and inconsistent behavior.

Religion, or anything else in life, should not be used to "buffer" this uncomfortable contact. Gurdjieff stated that much of human life is focused on activities that will anesthetize us from this unflattering process.

We must not only know about God but must also be brave enough to know ourselves! By studying Swedenborg and Gurdjieff we get a good dose of both!

Again, to make contact with and activate the sacred data in one's remains requires brutal self-examination and sincerity. Friction then results from the contact between the conflicting values lying deep within our psyche. This process of friction creates the "heat" that will forge our inner being into proper divine order (and fashion for us a spiritual body).

This is not a flattering process, but is necessary for each of us in order to find true humility and spiritual innocence. God's Spiritual Love and Goodness can only flow into innocence.

It is the division in the human psyche of the natural mind into external and internal functions (conscious and subconscious functions) that causes us to "fall asleep" as to our true duty in the world and disconnect us from our spiritual responsibility in life. Instead, we cultivate an upside-down view of reality (in which God does not play a major role). Gurdjieff gives this state of slumber a new and more contemporary twist by showing that this predicament leads to *suggestibility* and is why we go through life *hypnotized*!

By the way, because the activation of our remains causes us to look "upward" towards God (and not downwards towards worldly values), everything in our heart and mind becomes re-awakened and re-organized by this new heavenly (upwardly mobile) orientation. I cannot stress too strongly that it is only through the further evolution of one's God-given remains, by engaging in spiritual warfare, that new spiritual turf and heavenly bio-structure is created within us.

All the biblical battles in God's Holy Word address this *psycho-spiritual* turf war. We have to come out of our slumber and join God in this fight.

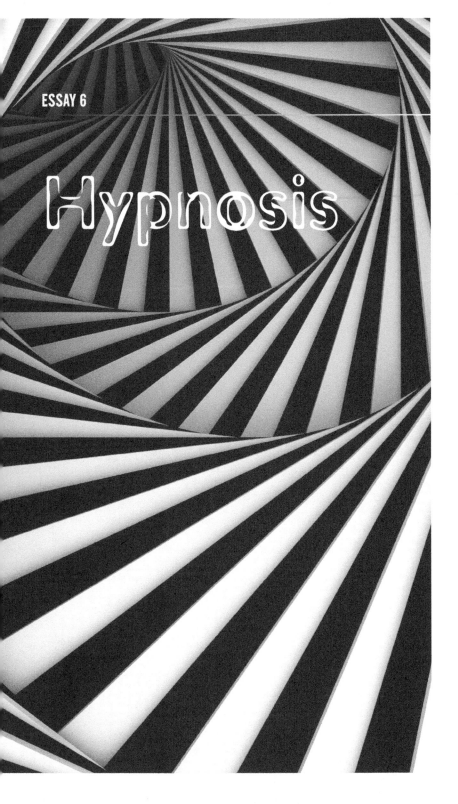

# Hypnosis

The term hypnosis was not coined during Swedenborg's life but he certainly understood its unique dynamics and how trance-states were created in the *divided* mind. Gurdjieff, being more contemporary, was able to explain this phenomenon more directly and using a more recognizable language.

The startling message of both seers is that the Lord did not simply come into the world to miraculously wipe away our sins but to *de-hypnotize* men and women. Without proper spiritual orientation, men and women are only capable of viewing reality upside-down, that is, as *fantasy*. One of the most striking strategies by the Lord to bust through the self-delusion of the human habitual mind and its limited consciousness was to warn us against finger-pointing and to concentrate on our own character faults.

The Bible has numerous passages warning people to "wake up" and "sleep not." This warning makes no sense unless it refers to a condition of the human mind—like being "asleep at the wheel." Humans go through life in a trance—that is why we often sense life as unreal or crazy.

This trance is the result of our inner being going into a "state of slumber" while the fabricated external personality we form in the world takes over for us. (This slumber of our inner essence is also the symbolic message behind the Fairy Tale *Sleeping Beauty*.) The Lord wants to snap us out of this sub-human and trance-like condition. This puts a whole new twist on acquiring a heavenly life. In fact, it challenges us to learn more about the nuts and bolts of the human intellect.

Swedenborg and Gurdjieff discovered that the human intellect consisted of a *sandwiching* of discrete, multi-leveled functions. Memory operates on one level, the imagination on another, and reasoning on yet another distinct (and more interior) level. In a nutshell, according to our passions or the manipulations from other people one of these distinct mental functions can be more intensely influenced and brought forward as other functions are shut down (flattery causes such a phenomenon). The brain can do this because the winding, serpentine structure of its neural networks can be crimped and collapse while other lobes, and areas can continue to expand (unfurl their fibers) and thus function more fully.

I cannot overly stress the importance of knowing that this process of disconnection can occur between distinct substrates in the neuron or brain cell itself. The function of memory, or imagination or reasoning that occupies these distinct substrates can therefore be isolated, blocked or intensified, which keeps us vulnerable to suggestability and gullibility. (Modern neuroscience is beginning to suspect that the neuron has levels in its own structure, which make higher functions of rationality and abstract thought possible.)

There is another part of the mechanism behind this unfortunate isolation of our cognitive functions. Swedenborg and Gurdjieff both claimed that we had three types of "bloods" that fill and activate these different levels of our neuro-structure. By manipulating human emotions and expectations these distinct fluid-forces can enter or leave our various cognitive substrates, whereby one or more can be shut off while another increases its flow and the tempo of its operation. When one function operates at the expense of others we come into a limited state of consciousness or trance. This is hypnosis!

We can observe this process of trance by disconnection when we imagine being in another place. As the image of this other place (like Hawaii) is reproduced in the mind's imagination our ocular sight gets momentarily shut off as we move from one mental function to another. Try it. Clinical or "parlor room" hypnosis is simply an exaggerated or intensified form of this simple phenomenon.

The allurements of fashion trends, fads and our obsession with glamour and worldly fame and honors are some of the more overlooked and milder manifestations of human trance. But hatred and murder also emerge from our not having access to all our mental facilities—like being separated from reasoning and ultimately our relationship with God.

Disconnection of our discrete mental functions is theologically symbolized as a state of damnation.

Hypnosis is rarely discussed in the same sentence as spiritual salvation. So consider this topic as an "advanced" course for your further enlightenment.

The activation of our "remains" during spiritual regeneration de-hypnotizes us! It *disturbs* our inner slumber and *re-connects* us to all our psychic functions, inner and outer, resulting in an increased consciousness of reality and a new awareness of why we are in the world and our personal responsibility within it. (Laziness is our ignoble defense to protect the inner calm of our slumber.) This spiritual reconnection of our psyche during regeneration is why the Latin root for the word religion means to "bring together" or "bind."

Swedenborg often used the roots of a word's origins to make his point. Gurdjieff even stated that philology was more important than philosophy!

Let me leave you with two thoughts for your further contemplation. Gurdjieff discovered that ancient civilizations noticed, early on, the negative effect of the disconnection of functions in the human psyche and described hypnosis as "The-taking-away-of-responsibility."

All irresponsible actions require some disconnection between our psychic functions. This is why when we break into a rage we instinctively say that we "lost it," while others accuse us of abandoning reason.

Secondly, according to Swedenborg, the greatest process of re-connection in history took place with the Lord's *glorification*. Jesus was Jehovah in the flesh. This allowed God's holiness to conquer human flesh and its defectiveness. Through incredible temptations, the Lord successfully purged his phoniness (from Mary's genetic influences) and unified his natural human life with His divine inner spirit (Jehovah). This great secret was shared with a couple of the Lord's disciples on the road to Emmaus.

We humans must go through the same purging steps and combats as did the Lord when He was in the world—but on a much smaller and less intense scale!

It was through Gurdjieff's experiments with hypnosis on a wide range of people that he was able to confirm this spiritual process was, indeed, not taking place.

# Full
# Top-Down
# Regeneration

During the process of spiritual rebirth or spiritual evolution, a person's mind is *reformed* on the way up and a person's heart or will is *regenerated* on the way back down, so that external or natural things come to serve internal or heavenly things. This up-and-down movement can also be looked at as *analysis* and *synthesis*.

The most famous expression of this up-and-down process in Holy Scripture is symbolized by *Jacob's Ladder.*

Swedenborg describes the first upward movement as starting in the human corporeal memory—in which we have a simple love of acquiring or collecting knowledge, such as in childhood. Next, from a higher aspect of love and affection in later life, we aspire to understand what we know. Finally, from a more noble principle of love, we seek to be rational beings and find wisdom.

Here is where the pendulum swings and we begin to acknowledge from true wisdom the Lord God of heaven as the true source of all love and goodness— and not ourselves. (This is where innocence and genuine goodness begins.) Many intelligent people can't get past this point—they find this "pill" too bitter to swallow. But if one succeeds here, the pendulum swing takes a person from being rational from a purely worldly perspective (for the sake of reputation) to becoming *spiritually* rational—which is a whole new animal and a real *inversion* of one's true being! This crucial step requires the full acceptance of our dependence on God for acquiring anything real. From this newfound humility and sincerity we now explore our heart and intentions to identify what negative compulsions or agendas we harbor—that are in conflict with what we intellectually know to be spiritually true. Then, asking for the Lord's help, we begin to resist these inconsistencies and flaws of behavior. In the New Testament, this purging activity is referred to as "cleaning the inside of the cup."

As we identify and remove these hurtful and false notions from our lives, our good actions in life finally become *genuinely good* because we now understand what good really is—God acting through us.

Unlike the discussion of involution in Essay #1, this second part of the spiritual process is indeed "downward." But it's "downward" in a good way, because the new *spiritual will* developing deep within our cerebral/intellectual part, has successfully intercepted the process of influx on its way back down, causing the formation of new recipient organic forms that bring God's proper order to the lower succeeding bio-levels of our being. Our new regenerated will now works its way back down to reorganize and bring new spiritual life and genuine goodness to all our psycho-levels—the reasoning mind, the imagination, and memory, even to our outward bodily actions. This downward direction of the regenerated human heart is symbolically expressed by the "opening of the womb" and a "new begetting" (spiritual rebirth) referred to in Exodus 13:15 as translated by Swedenborg. In this new spiritual re-creation our lower, worldly faculties are twisted back into their proper alignment and now *serve* the regenerated will of the spirit.

But here Swedenborg makes a curious statement about how this downward movement is rarely fully completed by men and women on Earth:

*"It is difficult for the actual level of the senses, which is the lowest of the natural, to be regenerated, because it is completely filled with material ideas formed from earthly, bodily and worldly things. Therefore, the person who is being regenerated, especially at this day, is not regenerated as to the sensory level, but as to the [middle] natural level which is next above the sensory level, to which he is raised up by the Lord from the sensory level, when thinking about the true things and good things of faith."* (AC 7442[4])

Hmmm?

While this predicament still represents a successful divine "rescue" from our lowest sensory level, it is not the fullest degree of spiritual regeneration! I believe the obstacle to this completed state is our fabricated personality that is formed during life. But why is this psychic level rarely fully rehabilitated from its flawed and downward orientation? I was curious about this and on further study found out that the difficulty here is that this lowest sensual plane is intimately connected with our motor functions. In other words, when something is done often enough and becomes habit, it also becomes automatic—that is, second nature. (Remember that in Essay #5, I mentioned that continued lying and deceit created this unfortunate second nature in our outer or fabricated personality.) Because this second nature is so familiar to us, we rarely bring it under scrutiny like we do with our more blatant transgressions. So our "remains," which rely on self-examination, have difficulty penetrating to this lowest plane.

God's heavenly influx cannot easily penetrate automatic behavior.

Human oversight in this matter causes many of us to falsely believe that whenever we unexpectedly "snap back" at people we are simply having a "bad day," when actually it represents behavior powerfully ingrained in our human apparatus.

If Gurdjieff's system of personal transformation is more difficult than Swedenborg's, it is because he takes self-examination (self-observation and self-remembering) all the way down into our lowest mechanical or corporeal nature. Instead of just identifying obvious "sins" and evil motives, Gurdjieff's system also challenges us to look at the extent to which our behavior is purely mechanical and on automatic pilot. Many of our bad traits and laziness, through habit, have become locked into automatic behavior.

This is a real shocker to the human ego when a person observes the true extent of his or her mechanicality.

But it provides additional evidence that we have great need to embrace humility in God's world and gain a more visceral and complete comprehension of the true extent of our dysfunctional lives and the self-deception that keeps us from spiritual liberation.

For this reason Gurdjieff stated that his approach was extremely difficult and not for everyone. Gurdjieff's system tackles the spiritual regeneration of even this lowest, corporeal/sensual level with actual exercises and tasks! (He even tailored these exercises to the specific needs of individuals.) Swedenborg did not offer precise methods for optimizing self-examination. I will concede this to my Gurdjieffian teacher. However, Swedenborg provided detailed descriptions of the motivations, compulsions and qualities of damned souls in the spiritual world, so that we could more easily identify these inclinations and flaws within ourselves!

While salvation does not require the transformation of our lowest, corporeal level, it is indeed required for men and women in order to reach their full spiritual potential. I think the Lord God is placing His hope that the Holy City, the New Jerusalem, will be inhabited by at least some individuals who make a serious go for it.

# Swedenborg's Circle of Life
# &
# Gurdjieff's Enneagram

Emanuel Swedenborg was a scientist, turned theologian. During his lifelong search for ultimate truth he discovered that all things in the created universe obey the same rules.

This holistic dynamic led him to eventually discover the *science of correspondences,* by which things of the visible universe mirror things of heaven. With this special knowledge, one can decipher new levels of meaning and revelations from both Nature and from the otherwise mundane narratives of God's Holy Word.

Correspondences are the only rational way to prove the inerrancy and authority of Holy Scripture. It also provides the keys to unifying science and theology.

Swedenborg and Gurdjieff both declared that men *see everything but understand nothing.*

They both saw the proliferation of information and data in the world as having a suffocating effect on the human soul. Symbolically speaking, the dangerous inundation of data in the world is represented by the biblical flood in Genesis and the Great Dragon in the Apocalypse who spewed water from its mouth to drown the woman who had given birth to a special male child. God's universal truth lets us rise above this deluge of data, as symbolically portrayed in the divine specifications of Noah's Ark and the emergence of "dry land" on the third day of the Creation story. (Both the Ark and Dry Land refer to our "remains.")

Through Divine Providence, I believe Swedenborg and Gurdjieff succeeded in offering humanity the universal model for unveiling God's great truths in order to spare us from becoming swamped by otherwise unimportant "facts and stuff."

Swedenborg called the patterning principle or cosmic template by which all process is determined the "Circle of Life." This circular and periodic model of universal process is somewhat analogous to the notion of the modern Theory of Everything (TOE) by today's physicists—but extends to all topics of enquiry!

Rather than limiting itself to unifying relativity theory with quantum mechanics, the Circle of Life, if properly understood, can unify creation theory, evolutionary theory, poly-dimensional space, psychology, Bible interpretation and even spiritual salvation—seamlessly!

My personal investigations have led me to conclude that Swedenborg's Circle of Life is the same as Gurdjieff's *Enneagram*.

The biggest clue was that both men stated that all process *returns to their first principles*, like a circle. The illustration on the facing page shows that the Enneagram, indeed, takes the form of a circle.

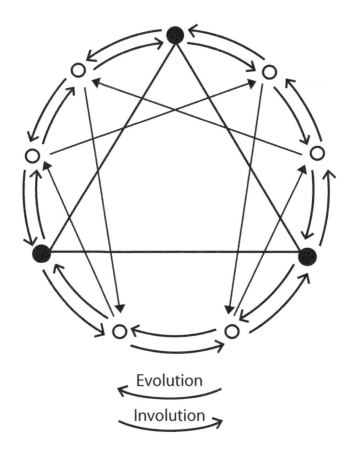

Evolution

Involution

Since the cosmological systems of both men embrace periodic or cyclic process, this suggests to me that their knowledge was not only identical but came from the same source—God. (In fact, Swedenborg's Circle of Life is mentioned in both his scientific and theological works.)

Let me describe Swedenborg's vision of his circular model of reality. I already mentioned that it was based on process returning to its first principles. He further said that all things comprise a *series* and each element of a series itself consists of a series (circles within circles). The parts or steps in each series represented the determining subjects by which a common equilibrium or harmonizing result is obtained. So every outcome or result of this holistic process gives us a replica or "an idea of the universe."

These series of steps, found within all coherent periodic units (systems) of process, were also called by Swedenborg "the subordination and coordination of things through successive and simultaneous order." The unfolding of each series is mathematically precise so Swedenborg also referred to his Circle of Life as the "mathematical philosophy of universals" and the "intuition of ends."

Both Swedenborg and Gurdjieff agreed that the periodic series of events following this circular pattern represented precise *centers-of-gravity* or nodes of stability that were mathematically arranged to produce concord and unity for the *whole*. (Such a model of relational holism would answer the current mystery in physics concerning the *thermodynamics of gravitating systems of order*, which would explain how nature grows coherent structure spontaneously.)

I suspect that the followers of Swedenborg and Gurdjieff will view my comparing of the Circle of Life with the Enneagram with some real skepticism (they already have). This is only natural, because my claim is a new and unexpected one to both parties. The closest a Swedenborgian scholar has previously come to constructing a circular model of universal process that I am aware of is in Carl Theophilus Odhner's book *The Golden Age*, in which he worked out a circular diagram of the Involuntary and Evolutionary trajectories of process in the Holy Word (pg. 25).

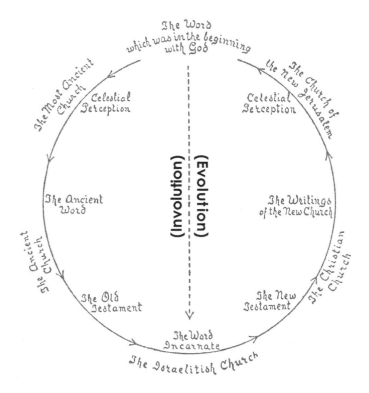

THE INVOLUTION AND EVOLUTION

OF

THE WORD.

*Notations on Involution and Evolution have been added for explanatory purposes and are not part of the original diagram.*

I was truly impressed by this "Swedenborgian" diagram even though it did not capture the full organic details of the divine design of a living God who works both *immediately* and *mediately*. God creates by organic steps and each organic step requires reciprocity (universal sharing—the essence of love). Odhner's diagram illustrates successive order. The enneagram illustrates both successive and simultaneous order (the inner connections of a system in its complex).

If the notion of arranging the architecture of Holy Scripture around a flowing circular construct seems odd, well, one of the assignments Gurdjieff gave his students was to place the Lord's Prayer around the enneagram.

Finally, both men did agree that this universal circular patterning principle was fully organic with strategic points where outer inputs (food) had to enter to keep the chain of events held together. Gurdjieff called this organic format the "reciprocal creation and mainte-nance of the universe." Swedenborg described it as "subsistence is perpetual existence, and conservation is perpetual creation." (WLG 57, pg. 119)

Gurjieffians might inwardly gloat that Gurdjieff provided them with a more finished model of this universal circular process, complete with several examples of how certain series of events could be properly placed on the enneagram (reproduced in Ouspensky's classic work *In Search Of The Miraculous*). True enough. But Gurdjieff has challenged the world to make new discoveries with it. I have seen limited attempts by Gurdjieff's followers to offer new renditions of the enneagram with the exception of John G. Bennett and Irmis B. Popoff's students. (So I offered several new renditions in my book *Proving God* to point readers in new directions.) Gurdjieff said that the ability of a person to put his knowledge on the enneagram determined how well he or she understood a particular subject. Swedenborg essentially said the same thing by claiming that a person's understanding depended on how well he or she could arrange their knowledge into a series.

But the main challenge in offering new insights into understanding the workings of the enneagram as the ultimate cosmological model of reality and how data can be arranged around its structure—or into a proper series—is that it represents "other-worldly" or angelic knowledge! Swedenborg's Circle of Life and Gurdjieff's enneagram represents the connate wisdom of the soul, which has a perception of Divine Providence operating within comprehensive wholes. As a result, this sacred knowledge is under the ultimate protection of God's Cherubim (like the Tree of Life), and its only access to humans is through intensive and uncommon spiritual evolution (it will not be distilled further by contemporary academia).

Gurdjieff even used an illustration of the enneagram containing the four living creatures (cherubs) of both Ezekiel's vision and vision of John in Revelation for the cover of a pamphlet promoting his *Institute For The Harmonious Development Of Man*.

Gurdjieff's system has been criticized for failing to produce other individuals on the same level of development as Gurdjieff. I suspect the same can be said about Swedenborg. Well, I believe no one has put him or herself under the same intensity of regeneration as they did. We put our own limits on how far we are willing to go. But we can always do better!

I really don't expect the Swedenborgian Church and the Gurdjieffian movement to officially join forces, but perhaps, more and more individuals from both camps will seek each other out and perfect their knowledge and efforts towards spiritual transformation.

The only real growth of a true church or esoteric school is spiritual growth.

# FURTHER
# EXPLORATION...

*Emanuel
Swedenborg*

# Further Exploration

*George Gurdjieff*

Emanuel Swedenborg and George I. Gurdjieff lived in different centuries, yet both claimed that a new paradigm shift was about to replace the current world-views concerning science and theology! The legacy these prolific seers have left us includes a wealth of resources on personal development for serious seekers.

For more information about the scientific and spiritual discoveries of Emanuel Swedenborg, and the life, teachings and work of George Gurdjieff, the following pages provide brief biographies and some links to aid you in your search.

# Emanuel Swedenborg

Emanuel Swedenborg (1688-1772) was a scientist who turned theologian in later life. From 1710-1745 he studied all the branches of science in his time and even invented new ones. He was the first anatomical investigator to formulate a neuron theory of the brain, which included deeper layers of neural scaffolding (substrates) that today's neuroscientists are now speculating. From 1745 to his death in 1772, Swedenborg responded to a higher calling and left behind his scientific projects. Instead, he created a complete systematic theology based on direct Divine revelation and exploration of the Spiritual World. Of interest to the author, Emanuel Swedenborg's scientific discoveries perfectly complement his later spiritual discoveries and may well hold the key to unifying all knowledge.

Swedenborg's vast written work includes some 200 titles on scientific and theological topics.

His most noteworthy theological books include:

Arcana Coelestia (Heavenly Secrets – 12 volumes )

Heaven and Hell

True Christianity

Divine Providence

Conjugial Love

Divine Love and Wisdom

# Further Exploration

### The Swedenborg Foundation
*The publisher of Swedenborg's writings in the U.S. Additionally, they publish and distribute some books applying these principles to contemporary life; also scholarly monographs.*
http://www.swedenborg.com

### Swedenborg Scientific Association
*Preserves, translates, publishes and distributes the Swedenborg's scientific works. They publish an annual journal of scholarly articles on related topics online.*
http://www.thenewphilosophyonline.org

### The Swedenborg Society, London
*A publisher, library and bookshop in London. They also organize lectures, conferences and exhibitions on relevant topics.*
http://www.swedenborg.org.uk

### The Online Swedenborgian Library
*Swedenborg's theological, scientific & philosophical works online and in a searchable form.*
http://www.swedenborg.org/library_list

### Staircase Press
*Elevate your mind with these independently published books that explore how all true knowledge is connected.*
http://www.staircasepress.com

### TheGodGuy Blog
*This lively blog is a discussion on new ideas concerning Science and Theology and their ultimate unification.*
http://thegodguy.wordpress.com

### Books, Articles, Sermons and Blogs
*Curated by Ian Thompson, this collection of links is based on the Writings of Emanuel Swedenborg.*
http://www.swedenborgstudy.com

# George Gurdjieff

George I. Gurdjieff (1866?-1949) was born in the Caucasus of the Near East. His father was Greek and his mother, Armenian. As a young boy he met many amazing individuals who were the surviving repositories of various ancient knowledge. Around 1915, Gurdjieff burst upon the European scene with an innovative system for tapping one's spiritual potentials by "combining the wisdom of the East with the energy of the West." His ideas included a universal science that embraced both the laws of nature and the laws of spiritual salvation. Gurdjieff's system, called the "Harmonious Development of Man," is viewed by the author as highly complementary to the scientific and theological ideas of Emanuel Swedenborg.

Gurdjieff's primary published books comprised a trilogy entitled *All and Everything*:

*Beelzebub's Tales to His Grandson*
*(All and Everything, First Series)*

*Meetings with Remarkable Men*
*(All and Everything, Second Series)*

*Life Is Real Only Then, When "I Am"*
*(All and Everything, Third Series)*

# Further Exploration

### The Gurdjieff Foundation
*The largest organization directly linked to Mr. Gurdjieff.*
http://www.gurdjieff.org/foundation.htm

### The Gurdjieff Society
*The activities of the Society are mainly in London. However, there are some groups elsewhere in the UK, as well as in some other countries, for which the Society is responsible.*
http://www.gurdjieff.com/

### Gurdjieff International Review
*A source of informed essays and commentary on the life, writings, and teachings of George Ivanovitch Gurdjieff.*
http://www.gurdjieff.org/index.en.htm

### Gurdjieff Legacy—The Teaching for our Time
*An independent exploration whose aim is to creatively apply Gurdjieff's seminal, esoteric teaching of self-transformation to contemporary life.*
http://www.gurdjieff-legacy.org

### Gurdjieff Internet Guide
*Gurdjieff Internet Guide contains interviews, articles, videos, book reviews, event listings and other material related to the teaching of G.I. Gurdjieff. You can add your own events and contribute reviews.*
http://www.gurdjieff-internet.com/index.php

### Bennett Books
*An online independent bookstore selling "books for serious seekers." A good source for hard-to-find Fourth Way books.*
http://www.bennettbooks.org

# About the Author

Award-winning author Edward F. Sylvia has had a most unique spiritual journey—a journey that is by no means over. Despite his worldly successes, his worst fears about himself came true during this spiritual quest. He discovered that he is a fraud!

Mr. Sylvia wants everyone to reach this same unflattering conclusion about themselves.

Obviously, the author, through his rare sincerity, is well-qualified to present such balloon-popping and ego-stomping news to the world. He has studied various approaches to spiritual transformation for over 40 years and has embraced the systems of Emanuel Swedenborg and George Gurdjieff. Both men are little known. Their ideas would remain strange and lost to the world if some individual did not emerge from their stinging influences to demonstrate their positive mutual effect—both now and for the hereafter.

Mr. Sylvia currently lives on an 11-acre homestead with his wife in southern Illinois. They have been married—and contributing to each other's spiritual growth—for 36 years. He is a past president of the St. Louis Publishers Association (SLPA) and enjoyed a long and prosperous career in advertising. The author feels that his successful marriage is his most important credential for attempting this current work.

# Notes on Images:

Many of the images and charts in this book have been specially created for this project. Others are public domain and still others are used with permission. We thank all contributors.

Cover photo by "xtrekx" via Veer.com.

Little hornets by "vnlit" via Veer.com.

Page 1: Rose. Plate 69. *Published by W. Gotis, Botanic Garden, Lambeth, Marsh. according to Act. Dec 1, 1788.*

Page 15: Original art "Bringing Swedenborg & Gurdjieff Together." ©2012 SCPD.

Page 25: Original art "Exodus from Symbolism," montage created from "Pegasus" by Corey Ford via Veer.com and "Crowd driven from Tomkins Square" by Frank Leslie, 1874; public domain via Wikimedia Commons. Montage ©2012 SCPD.

Page 63: Mother & child by FANCY Photography via Veer.com.

Page 73: Black & white spiral by Leigh Prather via Veer.com

Page 81: "Automoton" from the film *Hugo* ©2011 GK Films LLC. All rights reserved. TM/© 2012 Paramount Pictures. All rights reserved.

Page 89: Original art "Montage" created from details of ancient and contemporary sources, including Hawaiian petroglyphs, White Buffalo Medicine Wheel, Tibetan Wheel of Life, Celtic Tree of Life. All source images in the public domain.

Page 95: The "Involution and Evolution" of God's Holy Word from *The Golden Age* by Carl Theophilus Odhner ©1913 reprinted by THE ACADEMY BOOKSTORE, 1975. Used with permission.

Page 99: Star-forming region in the large Magellanic Cloud LH 95 as seen from the Hubble Space Telescope. © 2006 NASA, ESA.

Page 100: Painting of Emanuel Swedenborg by Swedish portrait artist Carl Fredrik von Breda in 1817.

Page 101: Photo of George Gurdjieff photo from http://www.gurdjieff.am/photos/photogallery-2.htm

page 106: Author photo ©2012 SCPD.

42934172R10068